God's Sound Bites! *

abbreviated in the book to G. S. B.

Written By

Dr. Sheila Hayford

Book Title: God's Sound Bites

Copyright © 2008 by Dr. Sheila Hayford

Published By: Dr. Sheila Hayford, What A Word Publishing and Media Group
http://www.whatawordpublishing.com
Email: info@whatawordpublishing.com

ISBN: 978-0-9914039-0-5

Printed in the United States of America.

Dedication:

- This book is dedicated first and foremost to Jesus Christ my Lord, the Alpha and Omega of my life
- and to my sister, Catherine, for her selfless love and support through the years. What a pearl!

Dr. Sheila Hayford.

Acknowledgments

I would like to thank and acknowledge:

- Bishop Doreina C. Miles, Senior Pastor of First Pilgrim Baptist Church for her prayers, love and support in appreciating God's call in my writing and in my life. You are a wonderful spiritual mother to many.

- Dr. Shelton Rhodes, Dean, College of Business, Delaware State University for his encouragement, example, integrity and leadership. You are a wonderful role model.

- Pastor Ellis Louden, Mrs. Katrina Smith and the ladies lunch bunch of Mount Zion A.M.E. Church, Mrs. Cecile Coleman, Mrs. Dorothy Coleman, Ms. Doris Cooper and Mrs. Maxine Lewis for their encouragement and support. Let God's good times roll!

- My fashionista friend and loyal supporter, Mrs. Charlotte Woods for her kind words of affirmation and her support. You have one "Hat" of a presence! Thank you for your positive reviews of my books.

- Wofa, Mercy and Ma' Flo for your friendship and love. You speak volumes by your actions. "Cousin" says thank you.

- My loving family; you are an everlasting gift from God. Indeed we say: the Lord God is always faithful. Always!

Dr. Sheila Hayford

Foreword:

Only Eternity Will Show!

As I wrote this book I thought about the person or persons who left the pamphlet on that chair in church. That was on the eve before Christmas several years ago. They had no knowledge of my life, my family or that the world would be so changed by that one action because the Lord used that pamphlet to bring me to eternal faith in Christ. I never had the privilege of meeting them, neither opportunity to thank them. And yet there are so many others like them. People who daily give of themselves as they help others fulfill God's purposes. How many people will we see in mansions in God's heaven that we never expected to meet? People who may have been discouraged because it did not appear in their everyday living that they were making a difference. Perhaps they did not live long enough to realize the influence and impact of their lives on this earth. Only eternity will show! God certainly has them in His book of Remembrance.

".and a book of remembrance was written before Him (God) for them that feared the LORD, and that thought upon His Name." Malachi Chapter 3 verse 16

Dr. Sheila Hayford

𝒢. 𝒮. ℬ. 1

Do not dwell on the past, unless you intend to live there.

Bible Reading

Philippians Chapter 3, verses 13, 14:

But this one thing I do, forgetting those things which are behind (past), and reaching forth (forward) unto those things that are before (ahead), I press (strive) toward the mark for the prize of the high calling of God in Christ Jesus.

G. OS. OB. 2

The further it seemed Joseph was from his dream, the closer he was to the palace.

Bible Reading

Genesis Chapter 41, verses 14, 39, and 40:

Then Pharaoh sent and called Joseph, and they brought him hastily out of the dungeon: and he shaved himself, and changed his raiment (clothes), and came in unto Pharaoh. And Pharaoh said unto Joseph.....Thou shalt be over my house, and according to thy word shall all my people be ruled: only in the throne will I be greater than thou.

G. O. B. 3

In the spiritual realm the normal thing is to talk to your mountains, that is, your obstacles and challenges; instead of letting your mountains talk to you.

Bible Reading

Matthew Chapter 21, verses 18, 19:

Now in the morning as he (the Lord Jesus) returned into the city, he hungered. And when he saw a fig tree in the way, he came to it, and found nothing thereon, but leaves only, and said unto it, Let no fruit grow on thee henceforward forever. And presently the fig tree withered away.

G. S. B. 4

The seed of the Word of God will change any situation. What soil are you planting that seed in?

Bible Reading
Matthew Chapter 13, verses 7, 8:
And some fell among thorns; and the thorns sprung up, and choked them: But other fell into good ground, and brought forth fruit, some an hundredfold, some sixtyfold, some thirtyfold.

G. S. B. 5

If God allowed it, it must be for my good.

Bible Reading

Romans Chapter 8, verse 28:

And we know that all things work together for good to them that love God, to them that are called according to his purpose.

G. S. B. 6

God has greater for me, in spite of me, for God's glory. Why? It is because it is based on what Jesus did for me.

Bible Reading

Romans Chapter 8, verse 1:

There is therefore now no condemnation to them which are in Christ Jesus, who walk not after the flesh, but after the (Holy) Spirit.

Isaiah Chapter 60, verses 1, 2, and 3:

Arise, shine; for thy light is come, and the glory of the LORD is risen upon thee. For...the LORD shall arise upon thee, and His glory shall be seen upon thee. And the

Gentiles shall come to thy light, and kings to the brightness of thy rising.

G. OS. OB. 7

One of the best gifts you can give a friend is your availability.

Bible Reading

Exodus Chapter 33, verse 11:

And the LORD spake unto Moses face to face, as a man speaketh unto his friend

James Chapter 2, verse 23:

…. Abraham believed God, and it was imputed unto him for righteousness: and he was called the friend of God.

G. O. B. 8

I want to live in the fullness of all God has for me.

Bible Reading

Jeremiah Chapter 35, verses 18, 19:

And Jeremiah said unto the house of the Rechabites, Thus saith the LORD of hosts, the God of Israel; Because ye have obeyed the commandment of Jonadab your father, and kept all his precepts, and done according to unto all that he hath commanded you: Therefore thus saith the LORD of hosts, the God of Israel; Jonadab the son of Rechab shall not want (will not lack) a man to stand before Me for ever

G. O. B. 9

Do not give up on your blessings for a morsel of lust.

Bible Reading

Genesis Chapter 25, verses 29, 30, 31, 32, 33 and 34:

Once when Jacob was cooking some stew, Esau came in from the open country, famished. He said to Jacob, "Quick, let me have some of that red stew! I'm famished!"...

...Jacob replied, "First sell me your birthright......Esau said, 'What good is the birthright to me? ..... So he swore an oath to him, selling his birthright to Jacob. Then Jacob gave Esau some bread and some lentil stew. He ate and drank, and then got up and left. So Esau despised his birthright. (NIV Translation)

Hebrews Chapter 12, verses 16, 17:

...godless like Esau, who for a single meal sold his inheritance rights as the oldest son. Afterward, as you know, when he wanted to inherit this blessing, he was rejected. He could bring no change of mind, though he sought the blessing with tears.

(NIV Translation)

G. S. B. 10

Did you know that sin could conceive? What are you conceiving?

Bible Reading

James Chapter 1, verse 15:

Then when lust hath conceived, it bringeth forth sin: and sin, when it is finished bringeth forth death.

G. OS. B. 11

Pray in seriousness and in truth.

Bible Reading

Zechariah Chapter 8, verse 21:

And the inhabitants of one city shall go to another, saying, Let us go speedily to pray before the LORD, and to seek the LORD of hosts: I will go also.

G. S. B. 12

Does God need you?

Bible Reading

Luke Chapter 19, verse 31:

And if any man ask you, Why do ye loose him? Thus shall ye say unto him, Because the Lord hath need of him.

G. O. B. 13

Oh Lord, make me indispensable to you!

Bible Reading:

John Chapter 1, verse 3:

All things were made by Him (Jesus Christ) and without Him was not anything made that was made.

Genesis Chapter 18, verses 17, 18, and 19: And the LORD said, Seeing that Abraham shall surely become a great and mighty nation....For I (the LORD) know him (Abraham), that he will command his children and his household after him, and they shall keep the way of the LORD, to do justice and judgment; That the LORD may bring upon Abraham that which He hath spoken of him.

G. S. B. 14

The Lord's victory is my victory.

Bible Reading

1 Samuel Chapter 2, verse 10:

The adversaries of the LORD shall be broken to pieces; out of heaven shall He thunder upon them: the LORD shall judge he ends of the earth; and He shall give strength unto his king, and exalt the horn of His anointed.

G. S. B. 15

God is showing me "Me".

Bible Reading

2 Kings Chapter 6, verse 17:

And Elisha prayed, and said, LORD, I pray thee, open his eyes, that he may see. And the LORD opened the eyes of the young man; and he saw: ...

G. S. B. 16

Do not force things to happen, let God make things happen.

Bible Reading

2 Kings Chapter 8, verse 6:

...So the king appointed unto her a special officer, saying, Restore all that was hers, and all the fruits of the field since the day that she left the land, even unto now.

G. O. B. 17

If God closed a chapter, do not pry it open.

Bible Reading

Genesis Chapter 19, verses 17, 26:

And it came to pass, when they had brought them forth abroad, that he said, ...look not behind thee,...lest thou be consumed.

But his (Lot's) wife looked back from behind him, and she became a pillar of salt.

G. S. B. 18

Jesus said, I will tell you what. This is how you know that you love me. Instead of telling me you love me all day, just keep my commandments.

Bible Reading

Micah Chapter 6, verse 8:

He hath shewed thee, O man, what is good; and what does the Lord require of thee, but to do justly, and to love mercy, and to walk humbly with thy God

John Chapter 14, verse 21:

He that hath my commandments, and keepeth them, he it is that loveth me

G. OS. CB. 19

I almost tripped doing what I was not supposed to do.

Bible Reading

2 Samuel Chapter 22, verse 37:

Thou hast enlarged my steps under me; so that my feet did not slip

Jude Chapter 1, verses 24, 25

Now unto Him that is able to keep you from falling, and to present you faultless before the presence of His glory with exceeding joy, To the only wise God our Savior, be glory and majesty, dominion and power, both now and ever. Amen.

G. S. B. 20

All because I said yes to Jesus and did it with great joy!

Bible Reading

Psalm 91 verses 14, 15 and 16:

Because he (or she) hath set his (or her) love upon me (the Lord God), therefore will I deliver him: I will set him up on high, ... and honor him. With long life will I satisfy him, and shew him my salvation.

G. O S. O B. 21

I am not going to blame God, I am going to thank God.

Bible Reading

Job Chapter 2, verse 10:

...In all this, Job did not sin in what he said.

(NIV Translation)

G. S. B. 22

The root cause of unforgiveness is pride.

Bible Reading

Romans Chapter 12, verse 3:

For I say, through the grace given unto me, to every man that is among you, not to think of himself more highly than he ought to think; ...

G. S. B. 23

Follow God's call in every situation.

Bible Reading

Revelation Chapter 10, verse 11:

And he (the angel of God sent by God) said unto me, Thou must prophesy again before many peoples, and nations, and tongues, and kings.

G. S. B. 24

Jesus' growth was linked to His obedience to His parents.

Bible Reading

Luke Chapter 2, verses 51, 52:

Then he (Jesus) went down to Nazareth with them (Joseph and Mary) and was obedient to them....And Jesus grew in wisdom and stature, and in favor with God and men.

(NIV Translation)

G. O. B. 25

Bring Jesus on the scene by sharing Him with others.

Bible Reading

Luke Chapter 24, verses 34, 35 and 36:

Saying, the Lord is risen indeed, and hath appeared unto Simon

And they told what things....

And as they thus spake, Jesus himself stood in the midst of them, and saith unto them, Peace be unto you.

G. S. B. 26

Jesus will give you the better ride!

Bible Reading

Revelation Chapter 6, verse 2:

...and behold a white horse: and he that sat on him had a bow; and a crown was given unto him: and he went forth conquering, and to conquer.

Revelation Chapter 19, verses 8, 14:

...for the fine linen is the righteousness of the saints ...And the armies which were in heaven followed Him (the Lord Jesus) upon white horses, clothed in fine linen, white and clean.

G. O.S. B. 27

Dear Lord Jesus, let me show my love for you in what I do, and the time I spend with you.

Bible Reading

2 Samuel Chapter 22, verses 1, 4 and 22:

And David spake unto the Lord the words of this song in the day that the Lord had delivered him out of the hand of all his enemies ...

I will call upon the LORD, who is worthy to be praised: ...For I have kept the ways of the LORD, and have not wickedly departed from my God.

G. S. B. 28

Satan's plans against me will come to nothing, while God's plans for me will come to fruition.

Bible Reading

Micah Chapter 4, verses 11, 12 and 13:

But now many nations are gathered against you. They say, "Let her be defiled, let our eyes gloat over Zion!" but they do not know the thoughts of the LORD; they do not understand his plan, he who gathers them like sheaves to the threshing floor. Rise and thresh, O Daughter of Zion, for I will give you horns of iron; I will give you hoofs of bronze and you will break to pieces many nations. You will devote their ill-gotten gains to the LORD, their wealth to the Lord of all the earth.

(NIV translation)

G. OS. B. 29

The devil is a sly fox. Don't fall for him.

Bible Reading

Hebrews Chapter 11, verse 25:

Choosing rather to suffer affliction with the people of God, than to enjoy the pleasures of sin for a season;

G. S. B. 30

Go and sin no more means go and do not repeat the same sin.

Bible Reading

1 Corinthians Chapter 15, verse 33, 34:

Do not be misled; "Bad company corrupts good character." Come back to your senses as you ought, and stop sinning;

...

(NIV translation)

G. S. B. 31

A child once told his brother he was going to keep the wrapper of the birthday gift I gave him so that when he was sixteen years old he could remember who gave it to him. He was only nine years old! If I was so touched by a child's gratefulness, how much more is God?

Bible Reading

Nehemiah Chapter 12, verse 31:

I had the leaders of Judah go up on top of the wall. I also assigned the two large choirs to give thanks ....

(NIV translation)

G. O.S. B. 32

Let God whisper sweet manythings into your ear.

Bible Reading

Daniel Chapter 12, verse 3:

And they that be wise shall shine as the brightness of the firmament; and they that turn many to righteousness as the stars for ever and ever.

G. S. B. 33

Do not let your emotions rob you of God ordained relationships.

Bible Reading

James Chapter 1, verses 19, 20:

Wherefore, my beloved brethren, let every man be swift to hear, slow to speak, slow to wrath: For the wrath of man worketh not the righteousness of God

G. S. B. 34

No wasted energies.

Bible Reading

2 Samuel Chapter 22, verses 35, 40:

He teacheth my hands to war; so that a bow of steel is broken by mine arms. For Thou (O God) hast girded me with strength to battle: them that rose up against me hast Thou subdued under me.

Isaiah Chapter 55, verse 2:

Wherefore do ye spend money for that which is not bread? And your labor for that which satisfieth not?

G. O.S. O.B. 35

She did not come to break your marriage, she came to test your marriage. Did you pass the test?

Bible Reading

Malachi Chapter 2, verse 15:

And did not He make one? ...And wherefore one? That he might seek a godly seed (children). Therefore take heed to your spirit, and let none deal treacherously against the wife of his youth.

2 Peter Chapter 2, verses 14, 19:

Having eyes full of adultery, and that cannot cease from sin; beguiling unstable souls: ... While they promise them liberty, they themselves are the servants of corruption: for of whom a man is overcome, of the same he is brought in bondage

G. S. B. 36

If the world did not set you up they cannot bring you down;

If God set you up no man can bring you down;

If God set you up then God can bring you down.

Bible Reading

Daniel Chapter 2, verses 20, 21:

Daniel answered and said, Blessed be the Name of God for ever and ever: for wisdom and might are His: And he changeth the times and seasons: He removeth kings, and setteth up kings: He giveth wisdom unto the wise, and knowledge to them that know understanding:

G. OS. CB. 37

God wants me in the know as to what God has for my life.

Bible Reading

Daniel Chapter 2, verse 23:

I thank Thee, and praise Thee, O thou God of my fathers, who has given me wisdom and might, and hast made known unto me now what we desired of thee: ....

G. S. B. 38

Does the word "lovely" define you?

Bible Reading

Psalm 90, verse 17:

And let the beauty of the LORD our God be upon us: and establish Thou the work of our hands......

G. S. B. 39

Old age is good.

Bible Reading

Zechariah Chapter 8, verses 4, 5:

Thus saith the LORD of hosts; There shall yet old men and old women dwell in the streets of Jerusalem, and every man with his staff in his hand for very age. And the streets of the city shall be full of boys and girls playing in the streets thereof

Psalm 91, verse 16:

With long life will I satisfy him, and shew him my salvation.

ᴂ. ᴂ. ᴂ. 40

Answer God's question! Will a man rob God?

Bible Reading

Malachi Chapter 3, verses 8, 10:

Will a man rob God? Yet ye have robbed me. But ye say, Wherein have we robbed thee? In tithes and offerings....Bring ye all the tithes into the storehouse, that there may be meat in Mine house, and prove me now herewith, saith the LORD of hosts, if I will not open the windows of heaven, and pour you out a blessing, that there shall not be room enough to receive it.

G. S. B. 41

I want my eyes to see clearly all God has for me.

Bible Reading

Revelation Chapter 10, verse 19:

Write the things which thou hast seen, and the things which are, and the things which shall be hereafter;

J. O.S. B. 42

When they found their compass, or sense of direction, they rejoiced.

Bible Reading

Matthew Chapter 2, verses 10, 11:

When they saw the star (their sense of direction), they rejoiced. On coming to the house (their destination, their purpose) they saw the child (Jesus Christ) with his mother (those assigned to him) and they bowed down and worshipped Him (God the Son).

G. S. B. 43

You tried but did you try hard enough?

Bible Reading

Hebrews Chapter 10, verse 24:

And let us consider one another to provoke unto love and good works:

G. S. B. 44

If you spend fifty-five minutes of your hour in prayer telling God about your problems, that is how big you have made your problems in relation to your God.

Bible Reading

Hebrews Chapter 11, verse 6:

And without faith it is impossible to please God, because anyone who comes to Him must believe that He exists and that He rewards those who earnestly seek Him (NIV Translation).

G. S. B. 45

Magnify your God in relation to your problems.

Bible Reading

Psalm 83, verse 18:

Let them know that You, whose Name is the LORD- that You alone are the Most High over all the earth.

G. O.S. O.B. 46

Let God melt your impossibilities.

Bible Reading

Hebrews Chapter 7, verse 25:

Wherefore He (Jesus Christ) is able to save them (us) to the uttermost that come unto God by Him, seeing that He ever liveth to make intercession for them.

G. S. B. 47

Protected in the blood of Jesus!

Bible Reading

Zechariah Chapter 2, verse 5:

For I, saith the LORD, will be unto her a wall of fire round about, and will be the glory in the midst of her.

G. O.S. C.B. 48

The more the devil tried to destroy Joseph, the further God pushed Joseph into his destiny.

Bible Reading

Genesis Chapter 50, verse 20:

You intended to harm me, but God intended it for good to accomplish what is now bring done, the saving of many lives. (NIV Translation)

G. S. B. 49

As long as we are on this earth, there is always something to do that is not <u>completely</u> completed.

Bible Reading

John Chapter 9, verse 4:

I must work the works of Him that sent me, while it is day: ….

Matthew Chapter 20, verses 6, 7:

And about the eleventh hour he went out, and found others standing idle, and saith unto them, Why stand ye here all day idle? They say unto him, Because no man hath hired us. He saith unto them, Go ye also into the vineyard; and whatsoever is right, that shall ye receive.

G. OS. CB. 50

How much do you know?

Bible Reading

Romans Chapter 6, verses 16, 17 and 18:

Know ye not, that to whom ye yield yourselves servants to obey, his servants ye are to whom ye obey; whether of sin unto death, or of obedience unto righteousness? But God be thanked...Being then made free from sin, we became servants of righteousness

Acts Chapter 12, verse 11:

And when Peter was come to himself, he said, Now I know of a surety, that the Lord hath sent his angel, and hath delivered me out of the hand of Herod, and from all the expectation of the people of the Jews.

G. S. B. 51

When you are tempted to harbor bitterness of heart, let mercy triumph over justice.

Bible Reading

Matthew Chapter 18, verse 33:

Shouldest not thou also have had compassion on thy fellow servant, even as I had pity on thee?

Habakkuk Chapter 3, verse 2:

...in wrath remember mercy.

Micah Chapter 4, verse 18:

Who is a God like unto Thee... He retaineth not His anger forever, because He delighteth in mercy.

G. O. B. 52

When Route 97 was under construction I fussed and fussed about what an inconvenience that was to drivers. Later when I moved to that area and used Route 97 back and forth to work, I realized that all the time I was fussing God was building that road for me. I should have been more thankful while it was undergoing construction. What is God building for you? It is better to start thanking Him now.

Bible Reading
John Chapter 14, verse 2:

In My Father's house are many mansions: ...I (Jesus Christ) go to prepare a place for you.

G. S. B. 53

The person God will tell the most about me and God's plan for me is "Me". Am I listening?

Bible Reading

Psalm 32, verse 8:

I (God Almighty) will instruct thee and teach thee in the way which thou shalt go: I will guide thee with Mine eye.

G. O.S. O.B. 54

If God is your teacher, the study material is designed to enable you pass the test.

Bible Reading

Psalm 73, verse 24:

Thou shalt guide me with Thy counsel, and afterward receive me to glory.

G. O.S. O.B. 55

Ask God for wisdom, understanding, discernment and direction.

Bible Reading

2 Samuel Chapter 5, verse 10:

And David went on, and grew great, and the LORD God of hosts was with him.

G. S. B. 56

Let God put you in the know, and you will no longer walk in the dark.

Bible Reading

Psalm 119, verse 105:

Thy Word is a lamp unto my feet, and a light unto my path.

G. O.S. O.B. 57

In the midst of the many voices in this world clamoring for your attention, take time to discern the distinctive voice of God.

Bible Reading

Joel Chapter 2, verse 11:

And the LORD shall utter His voice before His army: for His camp is very great: ...

G. S. B. 58

You can disagree with someone without taking offense.

Bible Reading

John Chapter 6, verses 60, 61:

Many therefore of his disciples, when they heard this, said, This is an hard saying; who can hear it? When Jesus knew in Himself that his disciples murmured at it, He said unto them, Doth this offend you?

G. S. B. 59

Winners win; because they risk what they have, to gain the better they do not have.

Bible Reading

Luke Chapter 8, verse 24:

For whosoever will save his life shall lose it: but whosoever will lose his life for My (the Lord Jesus') sake, the same shall save it.

G. S. B. 60

Do not give any human being God's place or God's position.

Bible Reading

Exodus Chapter 20, verse 3:

Thou shalt have no other gods before Me. (Jehovah God).

G. S. B. 61

In order to build up the body of Christ each of us must fulfill our God given assignment.

Bible Reading

Psalm 78, verse 72:

So he fed them according to the integrity of his heart; and guided them by the skillfulness of his hands.

G. S. B. 62

Jump into the water.

Bible Reading

Ezekiel Chapter 47, verse 12:

Fruit trees of all kinds will grow on both banks of the river. Their leaves will not wither, nor will their fruit fail. Every month they will bear, because the water from the sanctuary flows to them. Their fruit will serve as food and their leaves for healing. (NIV Translation)

ℊ. ℺. ℬ. 63

Protocol says: Do not be sad in the king's presence. What is your posture when you approach God?

Bible Reading

Ezra Chapter 6, verse 22:

For seven days they celebrated with joy the feast of Unleavened Bread, because the LORD had filled them with joy by changing the attitude of the king of Assyria, so that he assisted them in the work on the house of God, the God of Israel.

(NIV Translation)

G. S. B. 64

Did Jesus abandon His ministry because Judas betrayed Him? Neither should you.

Bible Reading

Hebrews Chapter 12, verses 2, 3:

Let us fix our eyes on Jesus, the author and perfecter of our faith, who for the joy set before Him endured the cross, scorning its shame, and sat down at the right hand of the throne of God. Consider Him (Jesus Christ) who endured such opposition from sinful men, so that you will not grow weary and lose heart.

(NIV Translation)

G. OS. B. 65

The godly and the ungodly can both be used by God; the ungodly to challenge the situation from the outside in, and the godly to change the situation from the inside out.

Bible Reading

Numbers Chapter 10, verse 32:

And it shall be, if thou go with us, yea, it shall be, that what goodness the LORD shall do unto us, the same will we do unto thee.

G. S. B. 66

Why didn't God part the Red Sea before the Israelites got there? It would have made the test of their faith too easy.

Bible Reading

1 Peter Chapter 1, verse 7:

That the trial of your faith, being much more precious than of gold that perisheth, though it be tried with fire, might be found unto praise and honor and glory at the appearing of Jesus Christ:

G. OS. OB. 67

Have patience with God.

Bible Reading

James Chapter 5, verses 7, 8:

Be patient therefore, brethren, unto the coming of the Lord. Behold, the husbandman waiteth for the precious fruit of the earth, and hath long patience for it, until he receive the early and latter rain. Be ye also patient; stablish (establish) your hearts: for the coming of the Lord draweth nigh.

Psalm 27, verse 14:

Wait on the LORD: be of good courage, and He shall strengthen thine heart: wait, I say, on the LORD.

Exodus Chapter 23, verse 30:

By little and little I (the Lord God) will drive them (your adversaries) out from before thee, until thou be increased, and inherit the land.

G. S. B. 68

A test is not designed to be easy.

Bible Reading

2 Chronicles Chapter 33, verses 12, 13:

And when he (Manasseh) was in affliction, he besought the Lord his God, and humbled himself greatly before the God of his fathers, And prayed unto Him: and He was entreated of him, and (God) heard his supplication, and brought him (Manasseh) again to Jerusalem into his kingdom. Then Manasseh knew that the LORD..... was God.

1 Peter Chapter 1, verse 7:

That the trial of your faith, being much more precious than of gold that perisheth, though it be tried with fire, might be found unto praise and honor and glory at the appearing of Jesus Christ:

𝒢. 𝒪𝒮. 𝒪𝒮. 69

The goal of the test is for you to pass the test.

Bible Reading

James Chapter 1, verse 12:

Blessed is the man who perseveres under trial, because when he has stood the test, he will receive the crown of life that God has promised to those who love him.

(NIV Translation)

G. O.S. O.B. 70

The thing about letting go of the past is that no one can do it for you.

Bible Reading

Philippians Chapter 3, verses 13, 14:

....but this one thing I do, forgetting those things which are behind, ...I press toward the mark for the prize of the high calling of God in Christ Jesus.

G. S. B. 71

The Word of God is in front of me, behind me, round about me and within me.

Bible Reading

1 John Chapter 1, verse 1:

That which was from the beginning, which we have heard, which we have seen with our eyes, which we have looked upon, and our hands have handled, of the Word of life;

G. S. B. 72

The Word of the Lord is surer than steel.

Bible Reading

2 Samuel Chapter 22, verses 33, 35:

God is my strength and power...He teacheth my hands to war; so that a bow of steel is broken by mine arms.

G. S. B. 73

Men may misjudge you but it is comforting to remember that God knows your heart.

Bible Reading

Job Chapter 42, verses 7, 8:

After the LORD had said these things to Job, He (The LORD) said to Eliphaz the Temanite, I am angry with you and your two friends because you have not spoken of Me what is right, as My servant Job has. ...My servant Job will pray for you, and I will accept his prayer and not deal with you according to your folly.

(NIV Translation)

G. S. B. 74

Serve others without being abnormally used (abused).

Bible Reading

Luke Chapter 13, verse 32:

He (Jesus the Christ) replied, Go tell that fox (King Herod), I will drive out demons and heal people today and tomorrow, and on the third day I will reach my goal.

(NIV Translation)

Acts Chapter 19, verses 11, 12:

And God wrought special miracles by the hand of Paul so that from his body were brought unto the sick handkerchiefs or aprons, and the diseases departed from them, and the evil spirits went out of them.

G. OS. OB. 75

Why does it seem there are many new churches and preachers springing up? It is because the earth shall be blanketed with the glory of God.

Bible Reading

Luke Chapter 2, verses 17, 20:

When they had seen him (Jesus), they spread the word concerning what had been told them about this child... glorifying and praising God for all the things they had heard and seen, which were just as they had been told. (NIV Translation)

G. S. B. 76

The fact that you are still alive means you came out on top. Visualize that!

Bible Reading

Job Chapter 42, verse 16:

After this (Job's troubles) Job lived an hundred and forty years, and saw his sons, and his sons' sons, even four generations.

G. O. B. 77

If your husband were the pastor would you treat him differently? If your wife was the pastor's wife would you treat her differently? If so, why the difference?

Bible Reading

James Chapter 3, verse 17:

But the wisdom that is from above is first pure, then peaceable, gentle, and easy to be entreated, full of mercy and good fruits, without partiality and without hypocrisy.

G. O.S. O.B. 78

If you thought about food all day would that make you grow? Why this question? It is because to grow in the Lord you must "eat" the Word of God by reading, understanding and applying it.

Bible Reading

Romans Chapter 15, verse 4:

For everything that was written in the past was written to teach us, so that through endurance and the encouragement of the Scriptures we might have hope.

(NIV Translation)

G. O. B. 79

Allow the Holy Spirit to be your instructor.

Bible Reading

Psalm 25, verse 4:

Shew me Thy ways, O LORD; teach me Thy paths.

John Chapter 16, verse 13:

Howbeit when He, the (Holy) Spirit of truth, is come, He will guide you into all truth: for He shall not speak of himself; but whatsoever he shall hear (from God), that shall he speak: and He will shew you things to come.

G. S. B. 80

Who said women could not build?

Bible Reading

Proverbs Chapter 14, verse 1:

Every wise woman buildeth her house: but the foolish plucketh it down with her hands

Nehemiah Chapter 3, verse 12:

And next unto him repaired Shallum the son of Halohesh, the ruler of the half part of Jerusalem, he and his daughters.

G. S. B. 81

Fortify yourselves with the Word of God.

Bible Reading

Daniel Chapter 2, verse 23:

I thank thee, and praise thee, O God of my fathers, who hast given me wisdom and might...

G. S. B. 82

Eliashib built the Lord's house and God had others build Eliashib's house.

Bible Reading

Nehemiah Chapter 3, verses 1, 21:

Eliashib the high priest and his fellow priests went to work and rebuilt the Sheep Gate. They dedicated it and set its doors in place ....Next to him (Baruch), Meremoth son of Uriah, the son of Hakkoz, repaired another section, from the entrance of Eliashib's house to the end of it.

(NIV Translation)

G. S. B. 83

Repair your own home!

Bible Reading

Proverbs Chapter 19, verse 18:

Chasten thy son while there is hope, and let not thy soul spare for his crying.

G. S. B. 84

The reason God asks us to fight and not grow weary is because of the payday reward we will receive at the end. Remember God's Word will always come to pass.

Bible Reading

Esther Chapter 9, verse 1:

….On this day the enemies had hoped to overpower them, but now the tables were turned and the Jews got the upper hand over those who hated them

(NIV Translation)

Hebrews Chapter 10, verse 36:

You need to persevere so that when you have done the will of God, you will receive what he has promised.

(NIV Translation)

G. S. B. 85

Are you going to believe the truth of God's Word?

Bible Reading

Hebrews Chapter 11, verses 7:

By faith Noah, being warned of God of things not seen as yet, ...prepared an ark to the saving of his house; ...and became heir of the righteousness which is by faith.

G. S. B. 86

In Christ I am a giant killer of the devil's dreams; and a giant builder of God's dreams.

Bible Reading

2 Chronicles Chapter 31, verse 21:

And in every work that he began in the service of the house of God, and in the law, and in the commandments, to seek his God, he did it with all his heart, and prospered.

G. O.S. O.B. 87

My prayer is that we will worship God as God desires and deserves because He is so worthy.

Bible Reading

Hebrews Chapter 1, verses 1, 2, 3 and 8:

God...Hath in these last days spoken unto us by His Son.... Who being the brightness of His glory, and the express image of His person, and upholding all things by the Word of His power, when He had by himself purged our sins, sat down at the right hand of the majesty on high;.....Thy throne, O God, is for ever and ever:...

Revelation Chapter 7, verse 12:

..Saying, Amen: Blessing, and glory, and wisdom, and thanksgiving, and, and power, and might, be unto our God for ever and ever. Amen.

G. S. B. 88

Our lives should be a perpetual dance before our God. Make God happy.

Bible Reading

Psalm 85, verse 10:

Love and faithfulness meet together; righteousness and peace kiss each other

G. S. B. 89

So what are you going to do with what you've got?

Bible Reading

Ezra Chapter 2, verses 68, 69:

When they arrived at the house of the LORD in Jerusalem, some of the heads of the families gave freewill offerings toward the rebuilding of the house of God on its site. According to their ability ...

(NIV Translation)

G. S. B. 90

God gives me things I did not know I had.

Bible Reading

Ephesians Chapter 3, verse 20:

Now unto Him (The Lord God) who is able to do exceeding abundantly above all that we ask or think, according to the power that worketh in us,

G. OS. B. 91

I want to receive all God's "yes" for me.

Bible Reading
Revelation Chapter 21, verse 7:

He that overcometh shall inherit all things; and I will be his God, and he shall be my son.

G. OS. B. 92

Blessed of God I am and cannot be cursed.

Bible Reading
Nehemiah Chapter 13, verse 2:

Because they ......had hired Ballam to call a curse down on them. (Our God, however , turned the curse into a blessing.)

G. S. B. 93

When people see me they see the glory of God.

Bible Reading

Exodus Chapter 34, verse 30:

And when Aaron and all the children of Israel saw Moses, behold, the skin of his face shone; and they were afraid to come nigh (near) him.

Acts Chapter 6, verse 15:

All who were sitting in the Sanhedrin looked intently at Stephen, and saw that his face was like the face of an angel (NIV Translation)

2 Thessalonians Chapter 1, verse 12:

That the name of our Lord Jesus Christ may be glorified in you, and ye in him, according to the grace of our God and the Lord Jesus Christ.

G. S. B. 94

It was there all along, but when the Lord revealed it to me I saw it.

Bible Reading

Acts Chapter 2, verse 28:

Thou hast made known to me the ways of life; thou shalt make me full of joy with thy countenance

G. S. B. 95

Do not let a lack of understanding take you or your family to an early grave.

Bible Reading

Proverbs Chapter 21, verse 16:

The man that wandereth out of (strays from) the way of understanding shall remain in the congregation of the dead

Job Chapter 17, verse 5:

If a man denounces his friends for reward, the eyes of his children will fail

Proverbs Chapter 6, verse 26:

For by means of a whorish woman a man is

brought to a piece of bread: and the adulteress will hunt for the precious life

G. OS. CB. 96

Take every Word of God with the intended mercy of God.

Bible Reading

Revelation Chapter 1, verse 3:

Blessed is he that readeth, and they that hear the words of this prophecy, and keep those things which are written therein: for the time is at hand.

G. S. B. 97

Life may not seem fair, but it does not have to be out of balance.

Bible Reading

Isaiah Chapter 40, verses 12, 18, 29 and 31:

Who hath measured the waters in the hollow of His hand, and meted out heaven with the span, and comprehended the dust of the earth in a measure, and weighed the mountains in scales, and the hills in a balance? ...To whom then will ye liken God? ...He giveth power to the faint ... they that wait upon the Lord shall renew their strength ...

G. O. B. 98

You are the only one of you there is!

Bible Reading

Acts Chapter 9, verse 15:

But the Lord said...he is a chosen vessel unto Me, to bear my Name before the Gentiles, and kings, and the children of Israel:

G. O. B. 99

Do you think Jesus will love you more because you fasted all the way? Remember, the fast is more for you than it is for Jesus.

Bible Reading

Colossians Chapter 2, verse 16:

Let no man therefore judge you in meat, or in drink, or in respect of an holyday, or of the new moon, or of the sabbath days:

G. S. B. 100

If you knock on doors for others, others will knock on doors for you.

Bible Reading

Proverbs Chapter 11, verse 25:

A generous man will prosper; he who refreshes others will himself be refreshed.

(NIV Translation)

G. S. B. 101

Keep keeping on!

Bible Reading

Revelation Chapter 2, verse 26:

And he that overcometh and keepeth my works unto the end, to him will I give power over the nations:

G. S. B. 102

If a word is a spoken thought, what are you thinking?

Bible Reading

Proverbs Chapter 13, verse 2:

A man shall eat good by the fruit of his mouth.....

Ecclesiastes Chapter 5, verse 2:

Be not rash (loose) with thy mouth, and let not thine heart be hasty to utter any thing before God: for God is in heaven, and thou upon the earth: therefore let thy words be few.

2 Chronicles Chapter 9, verse 23:

And all the kings of the earth sought the presence of Solomon, to hear his wisdom, that God had put in his heart.

G. S. B. 103

If you walk with Jesus, Jesus will walk with you.

Bible Reading

Matthew Chapter 14, verses 28, 29 and 32:

And Peter answered Him and said, Lord, if it be Thou, bid me come unto Thee on the water. And He (Jesus) said, Come. ....And when they were come into the ship, the wind ceased.

G. S. B. 104

The television crew and staff are paid to produce your favorite television shows. How much are you paying yourself to watch them?

Bible Reading

Ecclesiastes Chapter 3, verses 1, 6:

To everything there is a season, and a time to every purpose under the heaven:

A time to get, and a time to lose; a time to keep, and a time to cast away;

G. O. B. 105

It is not for you to worry about. It is for God to take care of. Release your burdens to the Lord.

Bible Reading

Ecclesiastes Chapter 5, verse 6:

Suffer not thy mouth to cause thy flesh to sin...wherefore should God be angry at thy voice, and destroy the work of thy hands?

G. S. B. 106

When I asked the right question, God gave me the right answer.

Bible Reading

Proverbs Chapter 18, verse 11:

A man's wisdom gives him patience; it is to his glory to overlook an offense.

(NIV translation)

G. S. B. 107

Look in the direction of your expectations.

Bible Reading

Numbers Chapter 32, verses 6, 7:

And Moses said unto the children of Gad and unto the children of Reuben, Shall your brethren go to war and ye sit here? And wherefore discourage ye the heart of the children of Israel from going over into the land which the LORD hath given them?

G. S. B. 108

Seems is what the eye says it looks like; Sound is what the heart hears God say about it.

Bible Reading

Matthew Chapter 9, verses 24, 25:

He (Jesus) said, "go away. The girl is not dead but asleep." But they laughed at Him.

After the crowd had been put outside, He went in and took the girl by the hand, and she got up. (NIV Translation)

G. S. B. 109

The devil wants me to finish the day down, God wants me to finish the day up.

Bible Reading:

Leviticus Chapter 26, verse 13:

I am the LORD your God, which brought you forth out of the land of Egypt, that ye should not be their bondsmen; and I have broken the bands of your yoke, and made you go upright.

G. OS. B. 110

Do not worship the vision; Worship the God who gave you the vision.

Bible Reading

Hebrews Chapter 13, verse 20, 21:

Now the God of peace....Make you perfect in every good work to do his will, working in you that which is wellpleasing in his sight, through Jesus Christ; to whom be glory for ever and ever. Amen.

G. OS. B. 111

Because of the power of God, I win.

Bible Reading

Revelation Chapter 12, verse 11:

And they (the saints of God) overcame him (satan) by the blood of the Lamb (Jesus Christ), and by the word of their (our) testimony...

G. S. B. 112

Why do you 'walk down" the mountain but "climb up" to the top of the mountain? Because climbing up is all the more difficult.

Bible Reading

Hebrews Chapter 12, verse 11:

No discipline seems pleasant at the time, but painful. Later on, however, it produces a harvest of righteousness and peace for those who have been trained by it.

(NIV Translation)

G. O.S. O.B. 113

Are we really talking to God when we interrupt our prayer to answer the phone or watch television?

Bible Reading

Revelation Chapter 15, verse 4:

Who shall not fear Thee, O Lord, and glorify Thy Name? for Thou only art holy:...

G. S. B. 114

How do you judge yourself?

Bible Reading

1 Corinthians Chapter 1, verse 18:

For the preaching of the cross is to them that perish foolishness; but unto us which are saved it is the power of God.

G. S. B. 115

While waiting for the bus I decided to take a break and browse in a nearby shop. After I returned in a few minutes the bus was gone. "That's not fair", I said, "after having waited so long." The Holy Spirit's reply was: "Where you at the bus stop when the bus arrived? That's the more important question."

Bible Reading

Matthew Chapter 25, verse 10:

And while they went to buy, the bridegroom came; and they that were ready went in with him went in with him to the marriage: and the door was shut.

G. S. B. 116

A church is supposed to be a candlestick providing light for the world to see.

Bible Reading

Revelations Chapter 1, verse 20:

......and the seven candlesticks which thou sawest are the seven churches.

G. S. B. 117

Obedience is its own reward.

Bible Reading

Jeremiah Chapter 26, verse 13:

Therefore now amend your ways and your doings, and obey the voice of the LORD your God; ...

G. O.S. C.B. 118

Righteousness is a position, right works is a manifestation.

Bible Reading

2 Thessalonians Chapter 1, verse 11:

Wherefore also we pray always for you, that our God would count you worthy of this calling, and fulfill all of the good pleasure of his goodness, and the work of faith with power:

G. S. B. 119

Walk by faith and see the manifestation in sight.

Bible Reading

1 Kings Chapter 18, verses 41, 42, 43, 44, 45 and 46:

And Elijah said unto Ahab, ...there is a sound of abundance of rain... And Elijah went to the top of Carmel; and he cast himself down upon the earth, and put his face between his knees, (prayed)

And (Elijah) said to his servant, go up now, look toward the sea. And he went up, and looked, and said, There is nothing. And he (Elijah) said, Go again seven times, And it came to pass at the seventh time, that he said, Behold there ariseth a little cloud out of the sea, like a man's hand...and it came to pass in the meanwhile, that the heaven was black with clouds and wind, and there was a great rain....And the hand of the Lord was on Elijah; and he girded up his loins, and ran before Ahab to the entrance of Jezreel.

G. S. B. 120

God had already forgiven David through Jesus Christ before he chose him to be king; so remember, nothing that you do or have done surprises God.

Bible Reading

Hebrews Chapter 11, verses 32, 33:

... of Samson ...of David also, and Samuel, and of the prophets: Who through faith subdued kingdoms, wrought righteousness, obtained promises, stopped the mouth of lions, ...

Psalm 139, verses 1, 3:
O LORD, Thou hast searched me and known me ... and art acquainted with all my ways...

G. S. B. 121

Do not hold onto a picture that does not exist.

Bible Reading

Matthew Chapter 28, verses 1, 5, 6, 8 and 9:

.......Mary Magdalene and the other Mary went to look at the tomb. ...The angel said to the women, "Do not be afraid, for I know you are looking for Jesus, who was crucified. He is not her; He has risen, just as he said.....So the women hurried away from the tomb afraid yet filled with joy....Suddenly Jesus met them, (NIV Translation)

Luke Chapter 24, verse 5:

...Why do you look for the living among the dead? (NIV Translation)

G. S. B. 122

God trusts Himself in me.

Bible Reading

Luke Chapter 1, verse 76:

And thou, child, shalt be called a prophet of the Highest: for thou shalt go before the face of the Lord to prepare His ways:

G. S. B. 123

When "I will" is not subject to "God's will" it is evil.

Bible Reading

Luke Chapter 12, verses 17, 18, 19, 20 and 21:

And he said, This will I do: I will pull down my barns and build greater....And I will say to my soul...eat, drink and be merry. But God said unto him, Thou fool, this night thy soul shall be required of thee......So is he that layeth up treasure for himself, and is not rich toward God.

G. O.S. B. 124

Satan in all his original beauty, prosperity and worship fell from such a position to so great a fall. That is an indication that beauty, prosperity and acts of worship will not of themselves keep us from falling. Only the blood of Jesus, and the power of God the Holy Spirit will.

Bible Reading:
Jude Chapter 1, verses 24, 25:

Now unto Him who is able to keep you from falling, and to present you faultless before the presence of His glory with exceeding joy, To the only wise God our Saviour, be glory and majesty, dominion and power, both now and ever. Amen.

G. S. B. 125

If God has called you to the top, do not let men seat you in the middle.

Bible Reading

Philemon Chapter 1, verse 16:

Not now as a servant, but above a servant, a brother beloved, specially to me, but how much more unto thee, both in the flesh, and in the Lord?

G. S. B. 126

It was a test. In other words God was going to use me as a test to see if we would pass the test based on the material He had just taught us in church. How many tests are passing us by?

Bible Reading

Mark Chapter 12, verses 30, 31:

And thou shalt love the Lord with all thy heart, and with all thy soul, and with all thy mind, and with all thy strength: This is the first commandment. And the second is like, namely this, Thou shalt love thy neighbor as thyself. There is none other commandment greater than these.

G. S. B 127

What a betterment difference a weekend makes.

Bible Reading

John Chapter 20, verses 1, 16:

The first day of the week cometh Mary Magdalene early, when it was yet dark, unto the sepulchre, and seeth the stone taken away from the sepulchre. Jesus saith unto her, Mary. She turned herself, and saith unto him, Rabboni; which is to say, Master.

G. S. B. 128

If Jesus walked by would we recognize Him?

Bible Reading

Matthew Chapter 25, verse 40:

And the King (Jesus) shall answer and say unto them, Verily I say unto you, Inasmuch as ye have done it unto one of the least of these my brethren, ye have done it unto me.

G. S. B. 129

The brethren in the parable should have been thankful that the Master chose them to work for Him and that the Master was going to reward them. Instead they began to compare their rewards with the other brethren and began to criticize their Master. Do we sometimes act like that?

Bible Reading

Matthew Chapter 20, verse 9:

And when they came that were hired about the eleventh hour, they received every man a penny. Romans Chapter 9 verse 15: ...I will have mercy on whom I will have mercy, and I will have compassion on whom I will have compassion.

G.O.B. 130

I see the glory of God but I am not a spectator.

Bible Reading

Exodus Chapter 24, verses 17, 18:

And the sight of the glory of the LORD was like devouring fire on the top of the mount in the eyes of the children of Israel. And Moses went into the midst of the cloud, and gat him up into the mount: and Moses was in the mount forty days and forty nights.

G.O.B. 131

It's already done.

Bible Reading

Romans Chapter 8, verses 29, 30:

For whom He did foreknow, He did also predestinate to be conformed to the image of His Son, that he might be the firstborn among many brethren. Moreover whom He did predestinate, them He also called: and whom He called, them He also justified: and whom He justified, them He also glorified.

G. S. B. 132

Oh that men would praise the God of all creation!

Bible Reading

Psalm 139, verses 14, 17:

I will praise Thee; for I am fearfully and wonderfully made: Marvelous are Thy works; and that my soul knoweth right well. How precious also are Thy thoughts unto me, o God! How great is the sum of them!

Psalm 19, verse 14:

Let the words of my mouth, and the meditation of my heart, be acceptable in thy sight, O LORD, my strength, and my Redeemer.

Prayer of Salvation

Dear Lord Jesus:

Thank you for the gift of each new day. It is a reminder of the life you have given me. I believe you died for my sins and rose again to bring me into the right relationship with God. I now give myself and my life wholly to you. Fill me with the Holy Spirit as you promised and help me live for you. Thank you for the gift of eternal life with you. Help me share this good news with others. In Your Name I pray, Amen.

I choose to remind myself of this special day. Date: _____

Bible Reading is helpful after praying the Prayer of Salvation. You may start by reading the Gospel of John and read a Chapter a Day.

THE VISION; OUR MISSION:

What A Word Publishing and Media Group is pleased to do our part to promote book writing nationwide. We believe that everyone has a story to tell; each story as varied as our life experiences. We believe that each story can have a positive benefit and, in some cases, a life changing effect on another person's life. We also recognize the barriers to book writing and publishing that may confront an individual. To this end we offer nationwide **Book Writing Seminars and Hands-On Workshops.** Our Book Seminars are designed to demystify the book writing and publishing process and our workshops are designed to provide hands-on experience in initiating the book writing process. We also offer Book Writing Seminars and Hands-On Workshops "ON LOCATION" so your group, church or organization's members can experience our book writing Seminars and Workshops at their location.

We also provide **Private Book Coaching and Book Editing services** for those who would like more individual and personalized attention and work with varying schedules and budgets.

Martin Luther King, Jr. so eloquently expressed in his "I Have a Dream" Speech the dream he envisioned for this nation. Our goal is to bring the book writing and publishing dreams of many to reality. To register for our Book Writing Seminars and Workshops, to request information on hosting a Book Seminar and Hands-On Workshop, or for private Book Coaching and Editing services, please contact What A Word Publishing and Media Group at info@whatawordpublishing.com or visit us online at www.whatawordpublishing.com You may also request information by calling 1-302-359-7710. We look forward to helping you achieve your book writing dreams!

Thank You!

www.ingramcontent.com/pod-product-compliance
Lightning Source LLC
LaVergne TN
LVHW021513080426
835509LV00018B/2495